SCENES
of America

NIAGARA FALLS

3410
April 22 1920

SCENES
of America

NIAGARA FALLS

DANIEL M. DUMYCH

Published by Arcadia Publishing
Charleston SC, Chicago IL, Portsmouth NH, San Francisco CA

Library of Congress control number: 2006929700

For all general information contact Arcadia Publishing at:
Telephone 843-853-2070
Fax 843-853-0044
E-mail sales@arcadiapublishing.com
For customer service and orders:
Toll-Free 1-888-313-2665

Visit us on the Internet at www.arcadiapublishing.com

On the cover: BOULDER BRIDGE, AROUND 1897. The lands surrounding the American Falls became a state park on July 15, 1885. Boulder Bridge connected the mainland to Willow Island. It was built with boulders collected from fields in the outlying areas of the city. (Author's collection.)

CONTENTS

INTRODUCTION

Among my earliest memories are recollections of a walk with my mother and sister along the Niagara River. We lived in the La Salle section of Niagara Falls on Stephenson Avenue and had walked down Sixty-third Street to get to the river's edge. To my eyes, things looked very odd. There was bare, yellowish, hard-packed earth beneath our feet and the massive tires of huge dump trucks were spouting dust as they rolled by, making me cough. My sister told me, in her best know-it-all way, that the machines were working on the "power project," a phrase that made no sense to me. Only years later did I learn that the Niagara Power Development was the force behind these historic movements, when new river shores were created, new highways and bridges built, the flow of Niagara's waters redirected, houses and buildings moved and demolished, and a new power station was constructed.

That, however, is not the focus of this book. My intention is to use photographs that document areas of Niagara Falls's history that I feel are especially important, and show the everyday scenes that are too often forgotten because they are so commonplace.

I think it is safe to say that there is a universal fondness for Falls Street among Niagara Falls's residents. Falls Street once acted as the corridor that linked the New York Central Railroad Station with Prospect Park. Out-of-town tourists who arrived by train were bound to patronize Falls Street businesses on their way to or from the falls.

The book celebrates one of our greatest local successes, the establishment of the Niagara Reservation in 1885. I'm glad to say that the park is still a success, more than 100 years after the fact.

The 1890s were a time of bold undertakings in America, a time of innovation and progress. Around this time, Niagara Falls established itself as a world leader in the development of hydroelectric and electro-chemical technology, and remained so for over a quarter of a century.

The village of La Salle, although so close to the thriving industrial areas along Buffalo Avenue, was quiet and rural, making it a perfect suburb for Niagara Falls. La Salle only flirted with industry briefly, possessing a button factory for a brief few years, a small automobile factory for several more, and a long, narrow canal leading to nowhere, built by a man named William Love.

The Niagara Power Project is Niagara Falls's most recent electrical upgrade. Photographs show the immensity of the project, and of the excavation and blasting work done on a gargantuan scale, much in the same way that Niagara's earlier projects were massive undertakings in their time.

This book is dedicated to my father, John Dumych (1915–1992).

ONE

"YEARS AGO"

THE BRIDGE FROM GOAT ISLAND TO BATH ISLAND, IN THE LATE 1870S. "Years ago," a report to the New York State Legislature read, "one of the loveliest features of the river was a little island with rocky shores overhung with foliage, in the dark shadows of which the waters whirled and sparkled as nowhere else." This island was now the domain of a paper mill, whose presence banished nature from its midst.

WILLIAM AUSTIN'S MILLINERY AND TAILORING ESTABLISHMENT ON FALLS STREET. William Austin's advertising proudly announced the location of the shop being, "in the center of the business portion of Niagara Falls." It carried a full line of millinery goods in the latest styles, as well as fancy goods. Austin, who was noted for his "excellence of workmanship and reasonable prices," attended to the tailoring aspect of the business himself. This photograph from the 1880s shows, from left to right, Anna M. Austin (William Austin's daughter), William Tugby (of Tugby's Mammoth Bazaar fame), and Miss Hart, a Chicago milliner. It was people such as these who founded and ran the shops that lined Falls Street—a street that would give so many people, not only from Niagara Falls but from the world over, bittersweet memories of that now vanished part of Niagara Falls.

A Woman and Child on a Goat Island Pathway, from a George Barker Stereoview Entitled "Listening to the Birds—Heart of Goat Island," c. 1890. Goat Island was (and still is) a place not only where one could go to enjoy nature in all its purity, but also to escape the city. The bridge to Goat Island was a gateway to a world unspoiled by the hand of man.

A View of C. O'Loughlin's Niagara Pharmacy, which was Located on the Southeast Corner of Second and Falls Streets, in the Gluck Building, c. 1893. This pharmacy was a popular place for soda water, phosphates, cherry flips, and other popular drinks, as well as Huyler's "celebrated" candies. The water used in O'Loughlin's soda fountain was considered exceptionally good, and came from a spring in the building's cellar.

A 1961 Photograph of Niagara Falls Power Company's Generator No. 2, which went into Operation in August 1895. When science-fiction writer H. G. Wells visited the power station, he was deeply moved. He would later write, "These dynamos and turbines . . . impressed me far more profoundly than the Cave of Winds. . . . They are will made visible, thought translated into easy and commanding things. They are clean, noiseless, and starkly powerful. All the clatter and tumult of the early age of machinery is past and gone here; there is no smoke, no coal grit, no dirt at all. . . . These are altogether noble masses of machinery, huge black slumbering monsters, great sleeping tops that engender irresistible forces in their sleep. . . . A man goes to and fro quietly in the long clean hall of the dynamos. There is no clangor, no racket. Yet, the outer rim of the big generators is spinning at the pace of a hundred thousand miles an hour. . . . All these great things are as silent, as wonderfully made, as the heart in a living body, and stouter and stronger than that."

THE "HIGH BANK," OR MILL DISTRICT, AS VIEWED FROM THE UPPER STEEL ARCH BRIDGE, JUNE 1896. The Niagara Falls Hydraulic Power and Manufacturing Company's Station No. 2 is visible at the bottom of the gorge, directly next to the mill tailraces. Upon completion, the powerhouse would be 170 feet long and 100 feet wide, with a power output capacity of about 34,000 horsepower. South of it is the Cliff Paper Company's powerhouse, which was in operation before either of the power companies. This wood pulp and newsprint manufacturer also had a building at the top of the gorge, which was connected to its lower building by an incline railway. Directly above, at the top of the gorge, is a large, shed-like building being erected by the Pittsburgh Reduction Company. This was its second plant; its first was on the lands of the Niagara Falls Power Company, on the upper Niagara River. The slide on the right of the photograph is a garbage chute, which dumped city refuse directly into the river.

THE FRENCH LANDING (OR LOWER LOOP) BRIDGE AT THE WESTERN END OF THE "THE LOOP," 1897. The Loop, now forgotten by most local residents, once ran eastwards, from the point where Seventh Street approached the river to the Port Day pier. This roadway, completed in 1897, was frequented by bicyclists (or "wheelmen" as they were known then), pedestrians, and visitors in carriages.

A GAZEBO NEAR THE AMERICAN RAPIDS, C. 1898. Mills and factories cluttered this site only 15 years earlier. With the establishment of the Niagara Reservation, all of the structures formerly here were demolished. They were replaced with a "natural" landscape carefully designed by Calvert Vaux and Frederick Law Olmsted.

THE HIGH BANK, OR MILL DISTRICT, AS IT LOOKED IN AUGUST 1899. In 1875, only one mill, Charles Gaskill's flourmill, occupied a site on the Hydraulic Canal basin, shown near the central portion of this photograph's right side. By 1899, almost all of the available space at the canal basin was utilized by industry. Along the top of the gorge were arrayed the Alloy Smelting Works; the Cataract City Milling Company; the Central Milling Company; the Cliff Paper Company; the National Electrolytic Company; the Niagara Falls Hydraulic Power and Manufacturing Company; the Niagara Falls Milling Company; the Oneida Community, Ltd.; the Pettebone-Cataract Paper Company; and the Pittsburgh Reduction Company, which had a second plant on the upper Niagara River. Nearby was the Niagara Falls Brewing Company. Surprisingly, directly adjacent to this heavily industrialized area were homes, hotels, restaurants, and small businesses. This condition must have been due to the industries locating along the basin after the residential area was already established.

A Crew Working at the Excavation of the Wheel Pit for Powerhouse No. 2 on New Year's Day, 1900. Construction of the power station went on night and day, in good weather and in bad. This photograph shows the very early stages of work on a wheel pit that, upon completion, would be 466 feet long and 17.5 feet wide, with an average depth of 177.43 feet.

TWO

A NEW CENTURY

SIGHTSEERS CROSSING A TEMPORARY WOODEN BRIDGE LINKING GREEN (FORMERLY BATH) ISLAND WITH GOAT ISLAND, 1901. In this photograph, one sees how very differently tourists of the past dressed for "taking in the sights." In 1900, work began to replace the Whipple truss iron bridges, which had linked the mainland to Green Island and Goat Island since the 1850s. The new, triple-arched bridges were concrete-steel arch bridges with stone facing, a gravel roadway, and granitoid sidewalks. Both had 20-foot wide roadways and two 10-foot sidewalks. The bridge from the mainland to Green Island was the longer of the two, being 393 feet long; the bridge from Green Island to Goat Island was 213 feet long. The total cost of the bridges, which stand to this day, was $102,070. The contract to build the bridges, which was signed on June 23, 1900, stipulated that the bridges must be completed by January 1, 1901. Labor unrest, however, set back the completion of the bridges to July 14, 1901.

A Night View of the Pan-American Exposition During a Thunderstorm, 1901. Buffalo, New York's "Pan" was originally slated for Cayuga Island, in what was then the village of La Salle. Pres. William McKinley came to the island on August 26, 1897, to initiate the project, but the venture came to a halt during the Spanish-American War. After the war's end, it was decided instead to locate the exposition on the north bank of Scajaquada Creek in Buffalo. The "Pan-American" was open from May 1 to November 1, 1901, and its predominant theme was electricity. Five thousand electrical horsepower of the Niagara Falls Power Company's power station was transmitted to the exposition, where it was used by more than 900 arc lights, 200,000 incandescent lamps, 400 miles of electrical wires, and 94 large, underwater, fountain spotlights. This photograph shows the focal point of the Pan-American, the 389-foot-high Electric Tower; in front of it are the Court of Fountains and the Ethnology Building. Near the base of the Electric Tower is an illuminated 74-foot-high replica of Niagara Falls.

A MODEL OF THE NIAGARA FALLS POWER COMPANY'S POWER STATION IN THE PAN AMERICAN EXPOSITION'S ELECTRICITY BUILDING. This photograph shows a portion of the Electricity Building's interior before the opening of the Exposition in May 1901. The building had displays dealing with magnetism, storage batteries, electrical measuring devices, incandescent and arc lighting, cooking and baking with electricity, electro-chemistry, electro-metallurgy, and electro-therapeutics.

THE EXPANSION OF THE CANAL, MAY 1901. By 1901, the Niagara Falls Hydraulic Power and Manufacturing Company, like the Niagara Falls Power Company, had requests for more power than it could provide. In response, it began an expansion program that called for a second powerhouse and a wider, deeper Hydraulic Canal that could provide the additional amount of diverted water that the new powerhouse required.

ICE AT THE BOTTOM OF POWERHOUSE NO. 2'S WHEEL PIT, FEBRUARY 11, 1902. The water seepage created not only impressive icicles, but also very difficult working conditions. This had been an especially savage winter. Toward mid-February, there were well-founded fears that the city's coal supply would become entirely depleted. Only a sudden improvement in weather conditions made it possible for the coal trains to reach the city in time.

THE DIRECTORS OF THE NIAGARA FALLS POWER COMPANY POSING ON THE STEPS INSIDE THE MAIN LOBBY OF POWERHOUSE NO. 2. Standing in the front row are, from left to right, Edward A. Wickes, Francis Lynde Stetson, Edward Dean Adams, and Darius Ogden Mills. Standing directly behind Mills is William B. Rankine. Edward Dean Adams, as president of the Cataract Construction Company, had precise ideas of what the powerhouse should be. He wrote, "It should be different (from others)—not a mill over a water-wheel with its old time mill-race and tail-race, but the housing of the torrents of Niagara, driven in its harness to hidden depths, where divested of its mighty power it speeds like a flash to distant use, long before its tail waters can return to their normal flow. It should be attractive, artistic in grandeur, dignified, impressive, enduring and monumental. The souvenir pictures carried away by the visitors should include one or all three of the powerhouses." This view of the powerhouse's interior proves that Adams achieved his goal.

THE "OLD STONE CHIMNEY" AS IT STOOD IN JULY 1902. In August 1902, the chimney, which had stood on the bank of the upper river for approximately 150 years, was taken down by the Niagara Falls Power Company, stone by stone, and moved to a new location on the property of the power company. A new factory, the Composite Board Company, was to be built on the land where the chimney stood, near the corner of Elizabeth Street (Eighteenth Street) and Buffalo Avenue; the chimney was moved to spare it from destruction. The old relic had a rich history, providing warmth and comfort to the men of Little Fort Niagara, and then, after the defeat of the French, the soldiers of Fort Schlosser. After the pullout of the British from the Niagara Frontier, the site was occupied by a tavern, which was burned to the ground by invading British forces in 1813. The chimney was moved twice more during the present century and now stands in what remains of Porter Park.

"THE NIAGARA," DESIGNED AND BUILT BY LA SALLE'S EUGENE ABBOTT KINSEY, SHOWN C. 1903. Kinsey began his work in the automotive field immediately after graduating from Cornell in 1901. That year, he demonstrated one of the early cars at the Pan American Exposition. Soon after, he established an automobile factory in the former J. B. Shantz Button Factory. Here, he manufactured a line of cars that included passenger and racing models.

AN ACCIDENT AT THE POWERHOUSE. Early on the morning of January 19, 1904, a mass of ice estimated to weigh between 30 and 40 tons broke away from the gorge wall above the Niagara Falls Hydraulic Power and Manufacturing Company's Powerhouse No. 2, and plunged through its roof, smashing it "as though it were an eggshell." This gigantic "icicle" began to form early in the winter at the waste weir of one of the mills at the top of the High Bank. Located almost directly above the powerhouse, it grew steadily, and soon alarmed power company officials. On the day before the accident, powerhouse workmen were told to be ready to evacuate the plant at a moment's notice. When the ice finally did crash into the powerhouse, the six men working in the building were able to escape safely. Four of the company's generators, shown in this photograph taken four days later, were put out of commission by the accident.

THE FALLS RESTAURANT, 15–17 WEST FALLS STREET, C. 1905. Situated one block away from the State Park Reservation, this restaurant featured a porterhouse steak dinner with potatoes, bread and butter, and tea or coffee for 45¢. Or, for a more frugal 25¢, one could dine on beefsteak, lamb chops, pork chops, or ham and eggs with bread and butter, tea or coffee, and potatoes.

51

THE FEBRUARY 25, 1907 FIRE AT THE ACKER PROCESS COMPANY. High winds, low water pressure, and a failure to immediately call the fire department doomed the plant. A falling brick wall killed one man during the fire. The plant's destruction was so great that the company chose not to rebuild its plant, forcing more than 250 workers to seek new employment. The Acker Process Company was located in an area bounded by Third Street, Walnut Avenue, the New York Central Railroad Tracks, and the Niagara Gorge. Going into operation in December 1900, it manufactured caustic soda, bleaching powder, tetrachloride of tin, tin crystals, and carbon tetrachloride, and purchased its electricity from the nearby Niagara Falls Hydraulic Power and Manufacturing Company. The electrolytic processes used in the plant were developed and patented by Charles E. Acker, who was also the company's first vice president. Shortly after the plant went into production, many neighborhood trees, shrubs, and plants began to sicken and die, and property owners lodged complaints and filed lawsuits against the plant's gaseous and particulate emissions.

A POSTCARD VIEW OF THE LITTLE NIAGARA RIVER FROM ABOUT 1907. It shows, on the left, Salt's Riverside Inn, which its advertisements claimed was a "refined and high class place." The restaurant's specialty was fish and game dinners. To the inn's right is a swing bridge that connected the mainland with Cayuga Island, on the far right.

Old Swing Bridge.
LaSalle, N.Y.

THE SCHOELLKOPF BRIDGE, AS IT LOOKED IN MAY 1909. Construction on this bridge, arching across the Hydraulic Canal, began in June 1906, and was completed in 1908. With a span of 110 feet, its 200-foot-wide roadway accommodated the traffic of both Third Street and Niagara Street. The three-story building on the corner stood on the site presently occupied by the *Niagara Falls Gazette*'s parking lot.

LA SALLE'S CAYUGA DRIVE SCHOOL. The school first opened its doors in 1909. The two-story brick building was built of cut stone and brick, with the bricks coming from the nearby Tompkins Brick Yard. In 1927, the school was enlarged, giving it 15 classrooms and a gymnasium. The school was closed by the Niagara Falls Board of Education in 1976 and was recently demolished.

60

S. Shearer's Groceries and Hardware Store, as Seen Around 1910. The store was located on the corner of Main Street (now Cayuga Drive) and Mang Avenue. The author wonders how successful Shearer was in selling hardware, with P. C. Goetzman's store across the street. Goetzman carried hardware, furnaces, stoves, glass, paints, oils, building supplies, and roofing, among other things. Goetzman's Hardware was a La Salle institution well into the 1970s.

THREE

GROWTH AND CHANGE

THE NEW YORK CENTRAL RAILROAD STATION, ON THE NORTHEAST CORNER OF FALLS AND SECOND STREETS, OCTOBER 1918. After being destroyed by a fire in early 1888, the depot was rebuilt for what was then the impressive sum of $20,000. Its builder remarked that he knew of no other depot along the New York Central Railroad's route that had so many fine features, not even the Grand Central Station in New York! Perhaps he might not have praised it so highly if a competitor had built the depot, but still, it had its charm. Entrance was gained to the station through a 24-foot arch, which lead into an oak vestibule with cathedral glass windows. The waiting rooms beyond it were wainscoted in antique oak, the walls, terra-cotta in color. On the northern wall was a large fireplace on whose mantle stood a clock that was saved from the depot when it burned. Many a farewell and greeting were given in this station, whose walls saw tears of sorrow and joy.

FALLS STREET, BETWEEN FIRST AND SECOND STREETS, C. 1918. On the right-hand side of the photograph is the Miller-Strong Drug Store; further down this block stand Amberg and Company and Beir Brothers. Across the street is Bowen's Pharmacy, which according to its advertising offered not only prescriptions but sodas, cigars, chocolates, and bon-bons. Beyond the pharmacy is Rae's Athletic Goods, the Harvard $1.50 Hat Shop, the Hotel Nassau, and the Fels Cafe.

THE IMPERIAL HOTEL, ON THE NORTHWEST CORNER OF FALLS AND SECOND STREETS, OCTOBER 1918. This hotel, which opened in July 1893, was at one time regarded as one of the finest hostelries in Niagara Falls. Its proprietors, one of whom formerly ran the Stephenson House in St. Catharines, Ontario, boasted that the Imperial was one of the very best $2-a-night hotels in the state. The bedrooms were furnished with antique oak furniture and heavy maquette carpets and the parlors, with satin upholstered furniture. The *Niagara Falls Gazette* of the day remarked that "every thing about the Imperial is nice—very nice." In the coming decades, many disembarking railroad travelers would stroll through the New York Central terminal, exit through its doors, and go directly across the street to the Imperial to "check in." When the number of rail travelers declined, so too declined the hotel's fortunes. It was demolished as part of the urban renewal program in 1971.

ERIE RAILROAD TRACKS, 1918. For much of their route through Niagara Falls, the tracks of the Erie Railroad lay between Eighth and Ninth Streets. This view, photographed from the Ferry Avenue bridge, shows the Walnut Avenue bridge crossing the tracks in the distance. In the 1960s, plans were made to build an arterial highway along this route, but a decrease in the city's population lead to the shelving of those plans.

THE ADAMS HARDWARE STORE IN 1918. The store sold everything from sporting goods to furnaces. Located on the corner of Cleveland Avenue and Main Street, it shared the city block with businesses such as the Imperial Tea Company, Housewife Bakeries, John Flynn and Son's boots and shoe store, Niagara Hat Cleaning and Restoring, Hager Wall Paper, Solomon Mokhiber's grocery, and David Bishara's shoe and cigar store.

THE PARK ENTRANCE, 1918. Although the city of Niagara Falls had existed for more than two decades, it still did not have any municipal parks in 1913. It was often discussed in city council meetings, but little was done to achieve this goal. Perhaps sensing indifference within the council ranks, Paul Schoellkopf purchased a tract of wooded land immediately east of the Niagara Falls Memorial Hospital, and transferred the deed to the city, with the understanding that this land was to become a park. The three-acre site was promptly designed and laid out by Fred W. Aigner, the city park superintendent. All entrances to the park converged upon the central area shown in this photograph. By the 1950s, the beautiful plantings shown here would be replaced by a tall cast-iron fountain, and the former flower beds graveled over. During the years that the park flourished, it served as a refuge for not only the public in general but also hospital visitors and high school students, whose school, Niagara Falls High, was located directly across Portage Avenue.

HOSE COMPANY NO. 6, AT HIGHLAND AND COLLEGE AVENUES, AS IT LOOKED IN 1918. The fire engine that the firefighters are posing on must have been a great source of pride for the department. Many cities still had horse-drawn fire apparatuses. Motorized fire engines were a relatively new development.

THE GROUNDBREAKING CEREMONIES FOR THE NIAGARA FALLS POWER COMPANY'S NEW POWER TUNNEL, APRIL 25, 1921. In 1918, the Hydraulic Power Company and the Niagara Falls Power Company were consolidated under the control and management of the Schoellkopf family and their associates. The resulting company retained the name of the Niagara Falls Power Company, and immediately embarked upon an expansion of the Schoellkopf Station. In December 1919, the largest generator in the world was put into operation at the power station. The $10 million construction project initiated at this groundbreaking ceremony would result in the creation of the world's largest hydroelectric station. The photograph shows Jacob F. Schoellkopf II standing with a shovel; to his left stand Schoellkopf family members and other company officials. Standing in the front row, smiling, with his arms folded, is Paul A. Schoellkopf, president of the Niagara Falls Power Company.

THE CONTROL ROOM FOR THE SCHOELLKOPF STATION, SEPTEMBER 1926. One can only imagine how futuristic this room must have looked to visitors in the 1920s and 1930s. The knowledge, too, that the switches, gauges, and levers in this room controlled the flow of all electricity made by this, the world's largest producer of power, made it even more awe-inspiring.

A Motor Camp Shown on a Late 1920s Postcard, Located on the Niagara and Buffalo Boulevard, near Evershed (now Fifty-sixth) Street. With rise of the automobile came a new form of recreation—automobile touring. In response, a new form of overnight lodging would arise—motor hotels, or, as we now know them, motels. Motels quickly evolved from pre-war motor camps after the end of World War II.

A Great Gorge Route Car Heading to the Whirlpool Rapids Stop, June 1927. The previous two stops for the Devil's Hole and Whirlpool were also popular stopover points for tourists, many of whom would bring a picnic lunch, relax, and be picked up by a later car.

EVERETT AND FRANK RAMSDELL. They were the two oldest employees of the Great Gorge Route. Photographed here in 1928, Everett (left), a motorman, guided the first car around the Canadian-American belt line in 1899, and also made the final trip on the line when it shut down in September 1932. As young boys, the Ramsdell brothers moved to Niagara Falls from Chicago with their family in the early 1890s. Everett was hired on to help erect poles along the railway's right-of-way during its construction, and a year after its completion, was given employment as a motorman. Frank, the younger of the two, obtained a job as a conductor in 1899. From 1920 until the Great Gorge Route's demise in 1935, the brothers worked together as the crew of car No. 1. When "notables" visited Niagara, it was the Ramsdells who were called on to man the luxuriously appointed Rapids car. Among their passengers were Pres. William McKinley, Prince Henry of Prussia, the King and Queen of Belgium, and Sarah Bernhardt.

WHEN ONE BRAGS, ONE NEEDS SUBSTANTIATION. Photograph-cards like this proclaimed, "I was at Niagara Falls! And here is the proof!" Little did it matter that this photograph was taken in front of a painted backdrop of the falls inside a tiny shop on Falls Street, rather than among rocks left behind by the falls as it eroded its way down the gorge. This card, too, illustrates the dilemma that experiencing the falls creates. Visitors want to enjoy the "naturalness" of the falls, and yet they also expect the modern conveniences they are accustomed to. Ever since the park's establishment by New York State in 1885, this has been a dilemma that park commissioners have had to grapple with. This pendulum of judicious balance swung to its outmost extreme in the late 1950s and early 1960s, when Robert Moses ran a parkway through the middle of Prospect Park and made a visit to the American Falls a brief drive-by experience. Happily, those days are over.

THE WHIRLPOOL RAPIDS STOP, JUNE 1928. This was one of the favorite "stop-over" points on the Great Gorge route. This party of tourists has just ascended from the observation platform below, on which was a rustic gazebo. The Great Gorge Route, which would operate under a deficit after 1930, went out of operation after a massive rock slide took out much of its trackage in 1935.

92

A GREAT GORGE ROUTE CAR, PULLING TWO EMPTY TRAILERS, C. 1932. Riding the Great Gorge route through the Niagara Gorge was for a time the second-most popular attraction for Niagara tourists. In the background, behind the front-end of the streetcar, is the Vernor's Ginger Ale shop at 16 Falls Street. A cold glass of sparkling Vernor's ginger ale was a "must" for summer time visitors.

MONTGOMERY WARD AND COMPANY AND NEISNER BROTHERS ON THE LEFT, SEARS, ROEBUCK AND COMPANY AND J. C. PENNEY COMPANY ON THE RIGHT, ON FALLS STREET BETWEEN PROSPECT AND MAIN STREETS, C. 1932. Sears and Montgomery Ward were both relative newcomers to Falls Street, both opening in 1929. Although overhead streetcar wiring and trackage are in plain view, this photograph shows a Falls Street increasingly dominated by the automobile. It also shows the evolution of retailing from small, specialized, locally owned businesses to national department store chains. Both the national chains and the public's new dependence on the automobile, which had parking requirements that streetcars never had, would lead eventually to the proliferation of suburban shopping plazas. These new shopping areas would sap the life out of downtown shopping districts all across the United States and Canada.

LOOKING EAST, DOWN FALLS STREET FROM RIVERWAY, JULY 1934. International Railway Company trolleys were still rumbling up and down Falls Street but they would be heard for only three more years. On the corner of the right side of Falls Street is a souvenir shop, the Pandora. Nearby are the Sandwich Shoppe (one can only wonder what was served there!), the American Automobile Association, the Community Chest of Niagara Falls, and the Niagara Falls Chamber of Commerce.

FOUR

TOWARD THE MODERN ERA

A Streetcar Shown in a Mid-1930s Photograph, Approaching Evershed Street on Buffalo Avenue. When the proposal to build the Niagara Falls and Buffalo Electric Railway was first put forward, its route ran directly through the center of La Salle, roughly .25 miles north of the New York Central railway tracks. Many private property owners refused to give the street railway right-of-way over their lands, forcing the railway to run its tracks along River Road (the present day Buffalo Avenue). Here too, they were opposed, albeit unsuccessfully, by La Salle farmers. The Niagara Falls and Buffalo Electric Railway went into operation on September 21, 1895. Its cars, which cost 50¢ to ride, were available every 15 minutes, and ran from Falls Street in Niagara Falls to downtown Buffalo, passing through La Salle, North Tonawanda, Tonawanda, and Kenmore on the way. The railway also provided "drawing-room cars," specially appointed cars that could be chartered for trolley and theater parties.

THE NORTHWEST CORNER OF WEST FALLS AND MAIN STREETS, MARCH 1936. On the corner is the Neisner Brother's 5¢ to $1 Store. Many years after this photograph was taken, the author would visit Neisner's and can still remember the aroma of the cashews and peanuts as they were roasted behind long glass counters just inside the right entrance to the store and the impressively long lunch counter, the creaking wooden floors, and the pet turtles that were for sale in the back of the store. Next door is Montgomery Ward and Company, the Park Restaurant with the International Billiard Room upstairs, and the Hotel Clifton, which also featured a restaurant named, appropriately enough, the Clifton Restaurant. Beyond the Hotel Clifton, on the corner where the Lockport and Niagara Falls Strap Railroad had its passenger station, and where only one year earlier trolley passengers boarded streetcars, is now located a Texaco gas station.

103

NIAGARA FALLS'S "GREAT WHITE WAY," FALLS STREET, AT NIGHT, AROUND 1939. The view of Falls Street looks west down the street. In the foreground are no-longer-used streetcar rails and bricked roadwork. The rails are paved over from the intersection of Third Street down to Prospect Park. In the distance is a bus pulled over in front of the train depot.

THE HIGH BANK IN 1954. The area had changed considerably from what it had been 50 years earlier. Formerly thick with mills and factories, the site was now largely grassed over. The last industry of significant size was the Aluminum Company of America's plant, which was located immediately north of the power station. The factory, which shut down in 1949, was razed by the Niagara Falls Power Company's successor, the Niagara Mohawk Power Corporation, in 1951 and 1952. All that remained from the "old days" of the Hydraulic Power Company were the buildings of the former Niagara Falls Brewing Company and the Niagara Falls Wallpaper Company, which built its sprawling complex on the site of the Acker Process Company's plant. A Howard Johnson's restaurant was now on the site of the Wm. A. Rogers factory. Within two more years, most of the Schoellkopf Station would be destroyed by a rock fall, and Niagara's history would undergo even greater changes, leaving only memories behind.

APR. 9, 1954   EXHIBIT E

A Bulldozer Clearing off Luna Island During the Summer of 1955. Luna Island had been closed to the public in September 1954, after the discovery of a 30-foot undercut in the Rochester shale beneath the observation area. Almost 16,000 cubic yards of rock was dynamited from the island during the remedial work, leaving it safe, but treeless and artificial looking.

THE SCHOELLKOPF DISASTER. On June 7, 1956, most of the Schoellkopf Power Station was destroyed when portions of the gorge wall above the power station broke away, dropping 120,000 tons of rock onto the power station. The collapse produced a shortage of low-cost power in the Niagara region, and electricity had to be routed in from other sources. Since the early 1950s, a consortium of five power companies had been negotiating to build a new power station near Niagara University, opposite Ontario Hydro's Sir Adam Beck Station. Talks were impeded by disagreement within government circles as to whether this development should be public or private. The Schoellkopf disaster compelled the government to come to a prompt decision. Pres. Dwight Eisenhower signed the Niagara Redevelopment Act on August 21, 1957, authorizing the New York Power Authority to undertake the project, but it was not until January 30, 1958, that the Power Authority received its license from the Federal Power Commission.

AN INTERIOR VIEW OF THE SCHOELLKOPF STATION, LOOKING SOUTH. This image shows how the rock fall destroyed the powerhouse. This powerhouse formerly extended for about 500 more feet, but the electrical equipment and the building itself now lay collapsed beneath the fallen rock. Miraculously, only one man was killed by the disaster.

THE SOURCE OF THE SCHOELLKOPF STATION DISASTER. In 1962, seismologist Dr. Austin McTigue revealed that there was little doubt that a September 20, 1946, earthquake led to the collapse of the power station 10 years later. The Schoellkopf Station, McTigue stated, rested on a fault or "joint" produced by the 1946 quake. Water, seeping from the Schoellkopf Station or Adams Station tunnels, slowly forced this joint open; ultimately causing the rock slide that demolished the power station.

BUILDING A NEW OBSERVATION TOWER, JUNE 1959. The Niagara Power Project entailed not only the construction of a power station, but also highways, parkways, parks, and the Lewiston-Queenston Bridge. At the same time that a 4,000-foot section of the Robert Moses Parkway was being built through Prospect Park, the Niagara Frontier State Park Commission was erecting a new observation tower.

THE NIAGARA RIVER, AUGUST 1960. The shoreline of the Niagara River underwent a drastic modification during the Niagara Power Project. The entire extent of the Robert Moses Parkway between the North Grand Island Bridge and the Loop was built on rock fill that was dumped into the Niagara River during the excavation of the power project's conduits and canals. The rock fill, which is light in color, is clearly visible in this photograph.

A Photograph Taken from the Power Station's Northern Abutment on a Snow-swept Day in February 1961. The image shows work taking place on the penstocks and in the transformer and generator area below. The 462-foot-long steel penstocks on the far end of the power station have already been encased in concrete; those in the foreground have been partially encased.

MEN OF AUTHORITY. Robert Moses, chairman of the State Power Authority (left), and Nelson A. Rockefeller, New York State governor and future United States vice president, holding the switch, were the two most powerful men in New York in 1961. Although Moses was an unelected public official, he at times possessed more authority than even the governor. On February 10, 1961, the two men stood side-by-side at ceremonies marking the first generation of commercial power at the Robert Moses Niagara Power Plant. At the elaborate observance, presided over by Moses, the invited audience gathered in Niagara University's gymnasium heard recorded messages delivered by Pres. John F. Kennedy, former presidents Dwight D. Eisenhower, Harry S. Truman, and Herbert Hoover, as well as the principal address, delivered by Governor Rockefeller. A specially commissioned musical composition by Ferde Grofe, Niagara Falls Suite, was performed by the Buffalo Philharmonic Orchestra. With that, Niagara entered a new age. Almost four decades later, its people have yet to find their place in it.

A VIEW OF THE CORNER OF SECOND AND FALLS STREETS, SEPTEMBER 29, 1964. The New York Central Railroad Station formerly occupied the empty lot in the foreground of this photograph. The parking lot across the street was the location of the Gluck Building, which was destroyed by fire in January 1959. This site was perhaps at one time the busiest intersection in the city.

THE ROBERT MOSES PARKWAY PASSING OVER WHAT WAS WILLOW ISLAND, C. 1964. Robert Moses, unlike landscape architects Calvert Vaux and Frederick Law Olmsted, felt that natural features needed to be steamrolled, blasted, or bulldozed to accommodate "progress." As part of the Power Project during the late 1950s and early 1960s, Moses dictated that a parkway be built upon construction fill deposited along the shore of the Niagara River between The Loop and the Grand Island Bridge. The parkway would not terminate at the eastern boundary of the Niagara Reservation, but would run directly through Prospect Park, continue under the Rainbow Bridge, and run along the top of the gorge northward to Lewiston. A visit to the American Falls became a 10-second drive-by experience for many. Those "old-fashioned" enough to still visit the park on foot were forced to walk up, over, and down steep, maze-like ramps that were built over the parkway. As for Willow Island and its Boulder Bridge, they were obliterated because they stood in the path of the parkway.

Arcadia Publishing is the leading local history publisher in the United States. With more than 3,000 titles in print and hundreds of new titles released every year, Arcadia has extensive specialized experience chronicling the history of communities and celebrating America's hidden stories, bringing to life people, places, and events from the past. To discover the history of other communities across the nation, please visit:

www.arcadiapublishing.com

Customized search tools allow you to find regional history books about the town where you grew up, the cities where your friends and relatives live, the town where your parents met, or even that retirement spot you've been dreaming of. The Arcadia Web site also provides history lovers with exclusive deals, advanced notice of new titles, e-mail alerts of author events, and much more.